curious about

DRAGSTERS

BY RACHEL GRACK

AMICUS

What are you

curious about?

CHAPTER **3** THREE

On the Dragstrip
PAGE
14

Curious About is published by
Amicus
P.O. Box 227
Mankato, MN 56002
www.amicuspublishing.us

Editors: Gillia Olson and Alissa Thielges
Designer: Kathleen Petelinsek
Photo researcher: Bridget Prehn

Library of Congress Cataloging-in-Publication Data
Names: Koestler-Grack, Rachel A., 1973- author.
Title: Curious about dragsters / by Rachel Grack.
Description: Mankato, Minnesota : Amicus, [2023] | Series:
Curious about cool rides | Includes bibliographical references
and index. | Audience: Ages 6–9 | Audience: Grades 2–3
Identifiers: LCCN 2020001133 (print) | LCCN 2020001134
(ebook) | ISBN 9781645491149 (library binding) | ISBN
9781681526812 (paperback) | ISBN 9781645491569 (pdf)
Subjects: LCSH: Dragsters—Juvenile literature.
| Drag racers—Juvenile literature.
Classification: LCC TL236.2 .K64 2023 (print) | LCC
TL236.2 (ebook) | DDC 629.228/5—dc23
LC record available at https://lccn.loc.gov/2020001133
LC ebook record available at https://lccn.loc.gov/2020001134

Photos © Alamy/ZUMA cover, 1; Alamy/Southcreek Global/
ZUMApress.com 2 (left), 5; Shutterstock/Jaroslaw Kilian 2
(right), 9; AP/David Allio 3, 17 (top); Shutterstock/Gino
Santa Maria 5 (Funny Car); Wikimedia Commons/GSenkow
5 (stock car); Shutterstock/Phillip Rubino 5 (motorcycle);
Getty/The Enthusiast Network 6–7; Alamy/Matt Woods
10–11; Alamy/Cal Sport Media 12–13; Alamy/Action
Plus Sports Images 14–15; Shutterstock/Somchai Som 17
(Earth); Shutterstock/ChameleonsEye 17 (roller coaster);
Shutterstock/3Dsculptor 17 (space shuttle); Shutterstock/
Grindstone Media Group 18–19; AP/Chris Brown 21

CHAPTER ONE

What are dragsters?

They are super-fast drag racing vehicles. Most drag races are just 0.25 mile (0.4 km) long. Top Fuel dragsters top 330 miles per hour (531 kph) on the **dragstrip**. Races often finish within 7 seconds. Don't blink!

TOP FUEL 3.7 SECONDS

FUNNY CAR 3.8 SECONDS

PRO STOCK 6.5 SECONDS

PRO STOCK MOTORCYCLE 6.8 SECONDS

What was the first dragster?

Mickey Thompson's slingshot dragster was first. He built it in 1954. The driver sat behind the rear wheels. He was like a rock in a slingshot. Today, Top Fuel racers look different. Engines are in the back instead of in front.

A slingshot dragster sits at the start of a dragstrip.

CHAPTER TWO

What makes dragsters so fast?

Lots of power! Dragsters have big engines with **custom** parts. Top Fuel cars produce more than 10,000 **horsepower**. That's 50 times the power of common street cars!

DID YOU KNOW?
Dragsters go from 0 to 100 mph (161 kph) in 0.8 seconds!

Engines are rebuilt
after each race.

What kind of fuel do dragsters use?

A dragster's exhaust catches fire as it takes off.

None use ordinary gas. Top Fuel and Funny Cars burn nitromethane. This mix of strong chemicals was once used as rocket fuel. It gives a dragster explosive speed. The **exhaust** catches fire. Flames blast out the **tailpipes**!

DID YOU KNOW?
Exhaust flames burn at 7,050 °F (3,900 °C).

Do dragsters need special tires?

Their back tires are big, heavy **slicks**. The rubber is smooth. The slicks aren't filled with much air. This helps them really dig in. The tires **buckle** as the car takes off. Tires wear out fast. New slicks get put on every 4 to 5 races.

The walls of the slick buckle as the dragster takes off.

CHAPTER THREE

What's a drag race like?

The tires smoke as a driver speeds down the dragstrip.

Short but action packed! Drivers pull up to the start line. They watch the light stand, called a **Christmas tree**. Three yellow lights flash, then . . . green! The cars blaze down the dragstrip. A red light means the driver started too soon. They lose the race.

DID YOU KNOW?
Drag races are LOUD! A crew and driver wear earmuffs to protect their hearing.

How does it feel behind the wheel?

Drivers say it's like riding a rocket. Top Fuel cars take off at 5 **Gs**. Drivers feel crushing weight on their chests. They get dizzy. Sometimes, they black out. The **cockpit** heats up to 130°F (54°C). The roaring engine makes their bones rattle!

It takes guts to drive in a drag race.

2–3 Gs

3 Gs

1 G

DID YOU KNOW?

Gs are the force of gravity. How do Gs feel?
1 G = Normal Earth gravity
2–3 Gs = Amusement park rides
3 Gs = Spaceship lifting off
5 Gs = Dragster race

Two parachutes help a Top Fuel dragster slow down.

Why do dragsters have parachutes?

Wheel brakes won't stop the cars. They are moving too fast. Parachutes are key to a safe stop. Drivers let them go just before the finish line. Two drag chutes fly out. They quickly slow the cars.

What happens between races?

Pit crews get busy. Drag races are hard on engines. They only last one run. Crews must tear apart and rebuild them between races. These fast cars have speedy crews. Cars are ready to race in 40 minutes. Time to roll!

Neptune

A mechanic works on a dragster before a race.

ASK MORE QUESTIONS

At what age can you drive a dragster?

What does the big wing on the back of the dragster do?

Try a BIG QUESTION: What kinds of skills does it take to be a dragster driver?

SEARCH FOR ANSWERS

Search the library catalog or the Internet.
A librarian, teacher, or parent can help you.

Using Keywords
Find the looking glass.

Keywords are the most important words in your question.

If you want to know:

- if kids can drag race, type: KIDS DRAG RACING

- what the wings on dragsters are for, type: DRAGSTER WINGS PURPOSE

FIND GOOD SOURCES

Here are some good, safe sources you can use in your research.
Your librarian can help you find more.

Books

Dragsters by Thomas Adamson, 2019.

Dragsters by Wendy Hinote Lanier, 2017.

Internet Sites

NHRA: Jr. Drag Racing
http://jrdragster.nhra.com/
The NHRA is a national drag racing organization. Be aware of ads on the site trying to sell things.

NHRA Videos
https://www.nhra.com/nhra/videos
Watch drag racing videos online! NHRA videos showcase race highlights and the science of racing. Beware of ads that might try to sell things.

Every effort has been made to ensure that these websites are appropriate for children. However, because of the nature of the Internet, it is impossible to guarantee that these sites will remain active indefinitely or that their contents will not be altered.

SHARE AND TAKE ACTION

Ask a parent to look for races near you.
Most states have raceways. If you go, don't forget your earplugs!

Hold a pinewood derby car drag race with your friends.
Make a dragstrip in your backyard. Take turns, and see who wins! Experiment by racing on a sidewalk or other surface. Try making the cars heavier. What happens?

Go to an NHRA Jr. Drag Racing event.
Head to the pits to talk to racers and their families. Learn what it takes to be a drag racer.

GLOSSARY

buckle To give in or crumple from pressure.

Christmas tree A stand with two columns of lights that tell drivers when to go and whether they started too soon.

cockpit The place where drivers sit.

custom Not standard.

dragstrip The track on which dragsters race.

exhaust The waste gases of an engine.

G The force of gravity; gravity is the force that pulls things down toward the ground.

horsepower A unit of power measured by the power of horses.

pit crew Members of a drag racing team who repair the car.

slick A dragster tire with smooth rubber.

tailpipe A pipe where exhaust blows out.

INDEX

About the Author

Rachel Grack has been editing and writing children's books since 1999. She lives on a ranch in Arizona. Hot cars have always fired her up! At one time, she even owned a street rod—a 1965 Ford Galaxie 500. She loved cruising with the windows down. This series refueled her passion for cool rides!